Celts
art and identity

Ian Leins

The British Museum

This publication accompanies the exhibitions *Celts: art and identity* and *Celts* organized by the British Museum and National Museums Scotland.

Celts: art and identity at the British Museum (24 September 2015–31 January 2016) is supported by:

In memory of Melvin R. Seiden
Sheila M. Streek
Stephen and Julie Fitzgerald
Fund for the Future donors

Celts at the National Museum of Scotland (10 March–25 September 2016) is kindly sponsored by Baillie Gifford Investment Managers.

First published in the United Kingdom in 2015
by The British Museum Press
A division of The British Museum Company Ltd
38 Russell Square, London WC1B 3QQ
britishmuseum.org/publishing
Reprinted 2015

A catalogue record for this book is available from the British Library

ISBN 978 0 7141 2837 5

Designed by Will Webb Design
Printed in Italy by Printer Trento S.r.l.

The papers used by The British Museum Press are recyclable products made from wood grown in well-managed forests and other controlled sources. The manufacturing processes conform to the environmental regulations of the country of origin.

Front cover

Feeding birds and intricate interlace patterns adorn the Rogart brooch, an outstanding example of early medieval Celtic art from Scotland.

AD 700–800
Rogart, Highland
Silver, gilt, glass; D 12 cm
National Museums Scotland, Edinburgh

Back cover

Waterbirds with sharply hooked beaks emerge from ambiguous plant-like designs on the Wandsworth shield boss. This early masterpiece of Celtic art was cast into the River Thames during the Iron Age.

350–150 BC
River Thames at Wandsworth, London
Copper alloy; D 33.3 cm
British Museum, London

Title page

Torcs (neck-rings) were worn all across Europe in the pre-Roman period, but their shape, design and decoration varied. This recent hoard included distinctive Scottish and Irish 'ribbon torcs' and others that reveal Continental connections and influences.

300–100 BC
Blair Drummond, Stirling
Gold; D 15 cm (loop-terminal torc)
National Museums Scotland, Edinburgh

This page

The form and decoration of this curious knife suggest a stylised bird. Bronze was an unusual choice for a knife (most from this time were made of iron). It may have had a special function, perhaps associated with religious practices.

300–200 BC
Found near St Albans, Hertfordshire
Bronze; L 11 cm
British Museum, London

Contents

Introduction   4

1. A Connected Europe   12

2. Powerful Objects   18

3. The Impact of Rome   28

4. A New Christian World   38

5. Renaissance and Revival   52

Illustration Credits   56

Bibliography   56

Braganza brooch

Greek and Roman texts describe the Celts as fierce warriors. Although archaeology suggests there was no single Celtic people at this time, it is clear that the diverse communities of Europe were in regular contact, exchanging objects and ideas. Weapons and arms, similar to those carried by the tiny Celtic warrior on the Braganza brooch, have been found across much of Europe, perhaps pointing to the existence of a widely shared warrior identity.

250–200 BC
Uncertain provenance, Spain or Portugal
Gold; L 14 cm
British Museum, London

Introduction

The word Celt has had many meanings. It was first used as a label for outsiders, a shorthand to describe barbarian peoples whose lands lay to the north of the civilised Mediterranean world inhabited by the Greeks and Romans. In recent centuries the word has been actively claimed to express a sense of belonging. Today, many people living in Scotland, Ireland, Wales, Cornwall, Brittany and the Isle of Man define themselves as Celts, an identity shared by people in diaspora communities across the world. Languages, art, music, dance, sport and belief can be Celtic. This scope is a problem: there is no single Celtic people and no simple Celtic history. The focus of this book will be the distinctive decorated objects made over a period of 2,500 years: objects that we now call Celtic art. From these, we can learn about the different groups that have been called Celts.

The ancient Celts were first mentioned by Greek writers soon after 500 BC. For the historian Herodotus they were to be found near the source of the river Danube and in the Iberian Peninsula. Caesar, writing during the Roman conquest of Gaul in the 50s BC, described how Gaul was divided into three parts, only one of which was inhabited by Celts. This provides perhaps the most restricted definition, confining the Celts to central and western France. Each Greek and Roman author who mentions the Celts tells a slightly different story and all must be read with a critical eye. Theirs was an external view of a changing world that they only partly understood. As the people of Iron Age Europe left few written records of their own, we do not know how they would have described themselves.

As modern ideas of the Celt are intimately bound up with Scottish, Irish and Welsh identity, one feature of the classical texts is of particular interest: the people of Britain and Ireland were never described as Celts; they were the Brittanni and Hiberni. The word is also absent from the surviving literature of early medieval Britain and Ireland, which speaks of Gaels, Scots, Picts and Britons. In fact, it was not until the eighteenth century that the term Celt was first linked to the inhabitants of these islands. At this time scholars

'[a] fondness for ornaments … both torcs round their necks and bracelets round their arms and wrists …'
(Strabo, *Geography*, c. AD 17)

noted similarities between languages spoken in Brittany, Cornwall, Ireland, Scotland, Wales and the Isle of Man. This, they thought, was evidence for an original ancient language shared between Britain, Ireland and France. The people occupying these lands must have been the Celts recorded by Caesar. Their language could be given the name Celtic.

Antiquarians who were struggling to understand the prehistory of Britain and Ireland seized upon this new term, describing ancient stone circles, such as Stonehenge and Avebury, as Celtic temples (although we now know that they date to the third millennium BC, long before the first recorded mention of the Celts). Later, in the mid-nineteenth century, the distinctive decorated objects of Iron Age Europe and early medieval Britain and Ireland were labelled Celtic art for the first time.

Snettisham Great Torc

In pre-Roman Europe, torcs (neck-rings) were symbols of power and status. The Snettisham 'Great Torc' is a technological and artistic masterpiece, made from over 1 kg of gold and silver, incorporating 64 wires twisted into eight separate coils. The terminals were modelled in wax then cast in gold onto the ends. They are decorated with the distinctive curving lines and shapes of Iron Age Celtic art.

100–50 BC
Found Snettisham, Norfolk
Electrum (gold and silver); D 19.9 cm
British Museum, London

Ilam pan

The inscription on this vessel lists four forts on Hadrian's Wall. It may have been made for a Roman officer as a souvenir of his military service in Britain. These small pans are typically Roman objects, but the spiralling enamelled frieze shows the influence of local traditions of Celtic art.

c. AD 130–200
Ilam, Staffordshire
Copper alloy, enamel; D 9.4 cm
British Museum, London; Potteries Museum & Art Gallery, Stoke; Tullie House Museum & Art Gallery, Carlisle

Language and art

Elements of ancient languages that we now call Celtic can be recognised from Ireland to Turkey. They survive as fragmentary inscriptions, which reveal a vocabulary and grammar related to those of languages still spoken in Brittany, Cornwall, Ireland, Scotland and Wales. But the identification of a long-lived language family across Europe does not help us to define the identities of the people who used them. Today, we call these languages Celtic, but this does not link them to a single group, less still to the ancient Celts. The name has only been applied to these languages recently, and in any case a shared linguistic heritage need not reveal a shared cultural identity. The ancient Celtic languages may have been related, but they need not have been mutually intelligible. In the early medieval period, when we have more evidence at our disposal, it is clear that the Celtic languages are characterised by their diversity, not their unity. St Columba, travelling from the west coast of Scotland to the east in the sixth century, required an interpreter.

Art is the other strand of evidence that spans the 2,500-year period from the first record of the Celts to the present day. During this time, a series of enigmatic, abstract art styles flourished in Europe; we now call

these Celtic art. The earliest Celtic art objects appeared in Europe north of the Alps *c.* 500 BC. Over the next couple of centuries, similarities could be seen between decorated objects made from the Atlantic to the Black Sea. The decoration was abstract and ambiguous, with only suggestions of human and animal forms. This new art style was restricted to fine metalwork and to objects associated with the elites of Iron Age Europe. By the first century BC/AD, when much of Europe had fallen under Roman control, these styles became largely restricted to Britain and Ireland. Here, they continued to develop and were later fused with new traditions from the Germanic world and Christian Europe to create the distinctive art style of early medieval Britain and Ireland, which adorned the stone crosses, manuscripts and valuable metal objects made after *c.* AD 650. Ornate works of art, characterised by interlaced patterns and spiralling motifs, were made on the western edges of Europe for many centuries.

Before the nineteenth century antiquarians had not considered objects or art when they thought of the Celts, focusing instead on language and the monuments of deep prehistory. It was only in the 1850s that scholars established a link between the art styles of the Iron Age and early medieval periods, and applied the word Celtic to both. This development was driven by curators in Edinburgh and London who sought to reorganise the collections of the national museums, incorporating spectacular new finds such as the Battersea shield and the Hunterston brooch.

New discoveries flooded into museums as a result of the river dredging, railway construction and agricultural development of Victorian Britain. The swirling, twisting designs of ancient Celtic art objects were a particular source of inspiration for British and Irish jewellery designers who created new versions of ancient Celtic brooches. In the later nineteenth century a generation of artists and designers reinvented the Celtic art that they saw on these objects, as part of an art movement known as the Celtic Revival.

Many books on Celtic art have sought to show continuity from prehistory to the present day, documenting the survival and evolution of a single Celtic art. But this was not a single continuous developing tradition. In each period we can see widespread similarities, but also regional variation and innovation. The styles that we now call Celtic art sparked to life at moments of contact between cultures: between Europe and the Mediterranean world from *c.* 500 BC; between native Britons and Romans, both before and after the Roman invasion of Britain in AD 43; and between the Christian communities of Scotland, Ireland and western Britain, and their Anglo-Saxon neighbours, in the seventh century AD.

No consistent style unites Celtic art across two and a half millennia. Instead, smiths and artisans were inspired by older artistic traditions, which they repeatedly reinvented, fusing them with new, external influences. For example, Mediterranean naturalism was transformed into more abstract styles. Each of these Celtic arts allowed people to express their different identities, to understand their heritage and their place in the world.

'if you take the trouble to look very closely, and penetrate with your eyes to the secret of the artistry, you will notice such intricacies, so delicate and subtle, so close together and well-knitted … and so fresh still in their colourings that you will not hesitate to declare that all these things must have been the result of the work, not of men, but of angels.' (Gerald of Wales, Archdeacon and chronicler, describing an Irish manuscript, AD 1187)

Monifieth cross-slab

In the centuries following the end of Roman rule in Britain, local forms of Christian worship developed among the Celtic-speaking communities of Scotland, Ireland and Wales. Celtic art was reinvented at this time as part of the creation of new Christian identities. Artisans drew on their wide connections, blending older motifs with new designs. On this Christian cross-slab, the familiar curving shapes at the top and bottom were combined with interlaced patterns, which came from Anglo-Saxon England.

AD 700–800
Monifieth, Angus
Grey sandstone; H 76 cm, W 30 cm, D 9 cm
National Museums Scotland, Edinburgh

Queen Mary's harp

Made *c.* 1450, this clarsach or Highland harp was owned by an aristocratic Scottish family for many generations. The intricate interlace and beasts are inspired by Celtic art from early medieval manuscripts and stone crosses. Noble families in Scotland and Ireland commissioned works decorated in this style to make a statement about their ancestry and heritage. The oak case (opposite) was made for a similar harp and later used to display this harp. It is lavishly carved with modern interpretations of ancient designs. The display case was a product of the artistic movement known as the Celtic Revival.

Harp: *c.* 1450
West Highlands
Wood and brass; H 81.2 cm, W 51 cm
National Museums Scotland, Edinburgh

Case: 1904
Edinburgh
Wood and glass; H 115.5 cm, W 94 cm
National Museums Scotland, Edinburgh

Witham shield

Stylised cows' heads with bulging eyes stare out from the metal facing of this wooden shield. Metal objects decorated with Celtic art often include three-dimensional motifs like this, which were hammered from the back using a technique known as repoussé. The incised swirling lines on the circular boss are another key element of the Celtic art that flourished in Iron Age Britain and Europe.

300–200 BC
River Witham near Lincoln, Lincolnshire
Copper alloy, coral; H of shield 109.2 cm
British Museum, London

Flagon handle

Early Celtic art can be seen as a response to the art of the Mediterranean world, allowing the people of central and western Europe to express their different identities. Wine flagons made in northern Italy in the later sixth century BC often included the faces of gods and gorgons on their handles. The Basse-Yutz flagons were inspired by such vessels, but the realistic faces were replaced with stylised heads with curling moustaches and intense staring eyes.

400–360 BC
Basse-Yutz, Lorraine, France
Copper alloy, coral and glass; face 6.7 cm
British Museum, London

Shield fitting

Celtic art became increasingly stylised over time. This bronze shield fitting was made a century or two after the Basse-Yutz flagons. Curling tendrils decorate the central dome, while at the top a few simple lines suggest the expressive face of a human or divine being.

300–200 BC
River Thames near Wandsworth, London
Copper alloy; H 37 cm
British Museum, London

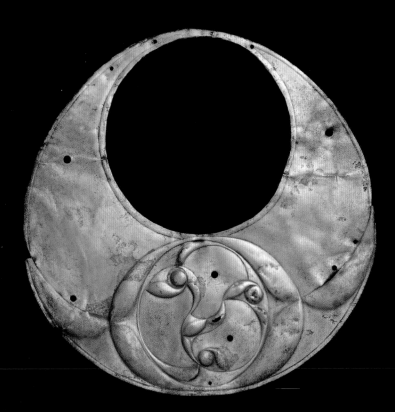

Decorated plaque

The beautifully balanced repoussé decoration on this plaque takes a three-legged or 'triskele' form that is typical of Celtic art. The motif may represent a stylised bird or animal. The precise function of the object is unclear, but it may have been a shield or chariot fitting.

150–50 BC
Llyn Cerrig Bach, Anglesey
Copper alloy; D 18.4 cm
National Museum Wales, Cardiff

Anklet (right)

Anklets like this one, with sculpted or three-dimensional shapes and spiralling designs, were produced across much of Europe from Germany to Hungary. This reveals something of the regular connections through which objects, ideas and technologies were exchanged.

300–200 BC
Plaňany, Bohemia, Czech Republic
Copper alloy; H 4 cm
National Museum, Prague

Sword scabbard (left)

Sword scabbards were often decorated with incised lines and hatching that formed sweeping plant-like designs. The decoration on this example clearly owes much to the wider development of Celtic art across Europe, but it is also part of a regionally distinct tradition particular to the north of Ireland.

300–200 BC
Lisnacrogher, Co. Antrim
Copper alloy; L 54.8 cm
British Museum, London

Linchpin (left)

Strange faces and beasts are often hidden within the ambiguous curving designs of early Celtic art. Simplified horse heads gaze out, wide-eyed, from either side of this linchpin from south-west Germany. Linchpins were used to secure chariot wheels on an axle.

300–200 BC
River Erms near Urach, Baden-Württemberg, Germany
Bronze, iron; H 10.7 cm
Württembergisches Landesmuseum, Stuttgart

2. Powerful Objects

The distinctive swirling Celtic art that developed from *c.* 500 BC rarely appeared on everyday objects. Yet its significance is clear from the arenas in which it was used: on weapons and warrior equipment, torcs and jewellery, vessels for communal feasts, and items used in relationships with the divine. Decoration gave objects special powers, saying something about the status of the wearer or user, or perhaps invoking the power of the gods.

Battles and skirmishes were a regular part of life, but they were as much about threatening display as actual physical violence. Some archaeologists have argued that the Battersea shield was a ritual object, being too thin to have offered effective protection in combat. But this is to ignore its bold decoration, and the animals and otherworldly faces hidden within its designs. The power of the Battersea shield may lie in its ability to dazzle and beguile opponents on the battlefield.

The finer detail of most Celtic art objects, however, would not have been visible from any distance. The twisting tendrils that adorn the top of the horned Waterloo helmet or the bird-headed horn terminals of the Torrs pony-cap reward only the closest inspection. Such items must have enhanced the status of their owners, who may also have believed that this form of decoration protected and empowered them.

Tableware embellished with Celtic art made a strong statement. At private gatherings important people showed off their social standing by serving their guests mead, ale or wine from luxury flagons and cups. Some vessels were imports from the Mediterranean, while others were local masterpieces decorated with Celtic art, such as the Clermont-Ferrand pottery.

The importance of these items is seen in their fate. Many of the most exquisite Celtic art objects that survive today were buried in graves or deposited as offerings in special places, particularly rivers. Their decoration gave them potency and made them worthy sacrifices to the gods.

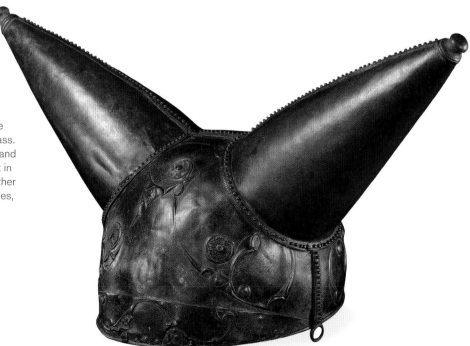

Waterloo helmet

When new, this bronze helmet would have been a golden colour, glinting with red glass. The elegant, curling patterns on the front and back of the helmet are typical of Celtic art in Britain before the Roman conquest. Whether it was used in battle or religious ceremonies, it would have served to demonstrate the power and authority of its wearer.

200–100 BC
River Thames near Waterloo Bridge, London
Copper alloy, red glass; W between horns 42.5 cm
British Museum, London

Torrs pony-cap

This extraordinary object was designed to be worn on a pony's head. The holes were for the pony's ears. It had long been thought that the horns were only attached after its discovery in the nineteenth century, but an entry in the *Caledonian Mercury* newspaper for 17 December 1812, recently uncovered in the archives, records the discovery of the cap with the horns already attached.

300–200 BC
Torrs, Dumfries & Galloway
Bronze; cap L 23.4 cm
National Museums Scotland, Edinburgh

'Those singularly beautiful curves, more beautiful perhaps in the parts that are not seen than in those that meet the eye, whose beauty is revealed in shadow more than form …'
(John Kemble, lecture to the Royal Irish Academy, 1857)

Battersea shield

Around 2,000 years ago people placed this ornate shield into the River Thames as a gift to their gods. Many such offerings were made in wet places, and the dead were sometimes cast into rivers. Some of the decoration can be seen as otherworldly faces. Depending on which way up and from which angle you view the shield, the same designs resolve into different creatures, some strange and menacing.

350–50 BC
River Thames at Battersea, London
Bronze, red glass; H 77.7 cm
British Museum, London

'the land produces neither wine nor oil, and as a consequence those Gauls who are deprived of these fruits make a drink out of barley which they call *zythos* or beer … The Gauls are exceedingly addicted to the use of wine and fill themselves with the wine which is brought into their country by merchants, drinking it unmixed…'
(Diodorus Siculus, writing between 60 and 30 BC)

Painted pottery

These pots feature contorted animals of
various shapes and sizes, creating striking
images. The animals are deliberately
hard to identify: many resemble deer, but
antlers, legs and ears are often stretched
or exaggerated. Vessels for communal
feasting were rarely elaborately decorated.
These ornate examples were perhaps
passed around a small group in restricted
gatherings. Embellishment, it seems, served
to distinguish the vessels used in these more
private settings.

150–100 BC
Clermont-Ferrand, Puy-de-Dôme, France
Painted ceramic; H of vessel on right 43 cm
Musée Bargoin (Musée Archaeologique),
Clermont-Ferrand

The Gundestrup cauldron

The cauldron is an extraordinarily powerful object that defies simple explanation. It is not Celtic, or at least not simply Celtic, but a product of the connected European world. It was discovered in a bog in Denmark, where it had been carefully dismantled and buried around 2,000 years ago. The findspot, in the tiny village of Gundestrup, lies well beyond the northern extent of the lands attributed to the Celts by Greek and Roman sources. Some of the metalworking techniques involved in the cauldron's production, as well as the choice of metal – silver – may identify its distant origins. A convincing case can now be made that the Gundestrup cauldron was manufactured in south-east Europe, probably in Bulgaria or Romania. The panels that adorn the cauldron, inside and out, are not decorated with the swirling motifs of Celtic art, yet the elaborate scenes show people wearing torcs as well as helmets ornamented with horns and animals, and carrying distinctive shields and war horns. These are the objects that we associate with the ancient Celts and which were often embellished with Celtic art. The cauldron is a visual feast. The outer panels show gods and goddesses, some attended by animals and diminutive human figures. Inside, fantastical beasts, deities and humans appear to play out scenes from long-lost stories and myths.

Gundestrup cauldron (opposite)

Gods and goddesses glare out from the cauldron's outer panels. Their staring eyes once held glass insets that would have glimmered in firelight. Their identities are lost to us, but their superhuman feats mark them out as powerful beings. One of the gods holds a pair of serpents. Human attendants braid the hair of one of the goddesses.

150–50 BC
Gundestrup, Jutland, Denmark
Silver; D 69 cm
National Museum of Denmark, Copenhagen

Outer panel from the cauldron (above)

Seven of the eight outer panels have survived. This torc-wearing deity is less animated than some of the others, who wrestle serpents and beasts, but his exquisite hairstyle and beard reveal the extraordinary skill of the cauldron's maker.

150–50 BC
Gundestrup, Jutland, Denmark
Silver; H 21 cm
National Museum of Denmark, Copenhagen

'For armour they use long shields, as high as a man … On their heads they put bronze helmets which have large embossed figures standing out from them and give an appearance of great size to those who wear them … Their trumpets are of peculiar nature and such as barbarians use, for when they are blown upon they give forth a harsh sound, appropriate to the tumult of war.' (Diodorus Siculus, writing between 60 and 30 BC)

Inner panel from the cauldron (above)

An antlered god sits crossed-legged at the centre of this scene from one of the interior panels. He holds a torc and a ram-headed snake, and is surrounded by a range of wild animals and a man riding a sea creature. The god's yogic pose and some of the animals on the cauldron hint at wider Asian influences.

150–50 BC
Gundestrup, Jutland, Denmark
Silver; H 21 cm
National Museum of Denmark, Copenhagen

Inner panel (opposite, above)

This panel shows warriors on foot and horseback, some wearing ornate boar- and bird-crested helmets. Three musicians are blowing boar-headed war horns (carnyces). A giant figure dips (or drowns) a warrior in a bucket-like cauldron. Is this a sacrifice scene? Or one showing the dead being brought back to life? We can only speculate as to the original meaning.

150–50 BC
Gundestrup, Jutland, Denmark
Silver; H 21 cm
National Museum of Denmark, Copenhagen

War horn (opposite)

Greek and Roman authors describe how the Celts made a terrifying wall of noise during battle, sometimes using a war horn called a carnyx. The head of this carnyx has the features of a boar. It is similar to the examples shown on the Gundestrup cauldron.

250–50 BC
Tintignac, Limousin, France
Bronze; H 1.80 m
Institut National de Recherches Archéologiques Préventives, Paris

3. The Impact of Rome

Contact with Rome transformed all aspects of life across Europe. Even before the Romans conquered an area, soldiers and merchants introduced fashions, ideas and technologies from the Mediterranean world. Revolutionary new types of objects, such as coins, were adopted by local communities. Portable and mass-produced, coins could carry powerful images and political messages to wider audiences than ever before. Faces and animals were more recognisable than those hidden in the scrolling patterns of earlier Celtic art, but coin designs were still deliberately stylised compared to the Greek and Roman originals.

In Britain, the Roman invasion of AD 43 created a cosmopolitan province where Roman and indigenous ways of life merged to create a unique culture. Towns and cities, amphitheatres and bathhouses appeared, along with new types of object. But while Celtic art died out on the Continent, abstract styles continued to change and thrive in Britain. People developed a distinctive British Celtic art, with complex interlocking curved lines and shapes. Some of the finest examples of this style are engraved on the backs of bronze mirrors. Skilled smiths and artisans explored the potential for combining Roman techniques with elements from earlier Celtic art.

In the battle for control that followed the Roman invasion of Britain, weapons and equipment were decorated with Celtic art. Innovative, colourfully enamelled designs were developed as an art of resistance that people used to emphasise their difference from the Romans. But allegiances were fluid, with some Britons choosing to fight alongside the Romans. The new styles were soon adopted by the conquerers themselves. Life remained very different in Ireland and northern Scotland. These areas were never conquered, but were still affected by the impact of Rome. On both sides of the Roman frontier in Britain, people wore jewellery that fused Roman and local designs, which served to express both Romano-British and non-Roman identities.

Opposite, left

Before the Roman conquest, communities from the Black Sea to the Atlantic minted their own highly distinctive coins. Many included stylised heads with elaborately curled hair. This head was based on that of the god Apollo, which appeared on coins of Philip II of Macedon (359–336 BC), but was deliberately rendered to cater for local preferences for stylised designs.

c. 200–150 BC
Fenny Stratford, Buckinghamshire,
Gold; D 26 mm
British Museum, London

Opposite, centre

Although the designs on coins were usually more naturalistic than those on earlier Celtic art objects, they retain a strong abstract element. Artists hid details within the features of a head. Here, an upside-down boar lurks behind the bulging cheek.

c. 200–100 BC
Lens, Pas-de-Calais, France
Gold; D 21 mm
British Museum, London

Opposite, right

On close inspection a boar in a dotted bubble can clearly be seen on the top of this realistic head. Tiny human heads were also connected to this by lines of beads, although they are not clear on this example.

c. 150–50 BC
Unknown findspot, probably
Brittany, France
Gold; D 21 mm
British Museum, London

Below

The design on this third-century BC silver coin from the Carpathian Mountains in Romania is instantly recognisable as a horse. It is more naturalistic than many early depictions of animals in Celtic art, but it retains a clear abstract flavour. The cartoon-like animal was undoubtedly designed to make the best use of the circular canvas of the coin.

c. 300–200 BC
Medieşu Aurit, Satu Mare, Romania
Silver; D 23 mm
British Museum, London

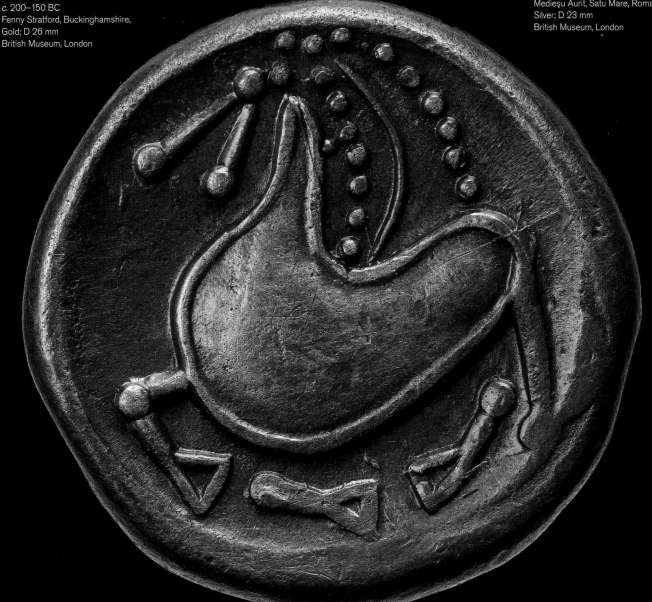

Stanwick horse mask (left)

From *c.* 100 BC, people often decorated objects associated with food and drink with human or divine faces, horses, boars, bulls and birds. This beautiful mount evokes a horse in a few sweeping lines.

AD 40–80
Stanwick, North Yorkshire
Copper alloy; H 10.0 cm
British Museum, London

Boar figurine (right)

The function of this small model boar is unclear, but its arched pose may suggest that it was attached to the top of a helmet. Some of the warriors on the Gundestrup cauldron wear helmets with decorative boars. These fierce wild animals may have been a symbol of protection or courage in battle in the Iron Age, appearing on shields and war horns. The naturalism of the boar shows the influence of more realistic Roman art.

100 BC–AD 100
Ashmanhaugh, Norfolk
Copper alloy; L 8.7 cm
Norwich Castle Museum

Cow-headed grinder (left)

Shortly before the Roman invasion of Britain in AD 43, new types of object appeared that reflected changes in how people dressed and presented themselves. Many of these items were decorated with animals. Grinders, used for preparing cosmetics, often feature stylised animal heads.

AD 1–100
Hockwold, Norfolk, England
Copper alloy; L of grinder 10.3 cm
British Museum, London

Aylesford bucket

Distinctive faces with impressive headdresses
decorate the rim of this bucket, which was
probably used for serving ale, mead or wine.
The burial that included the Aylesford bucket
also contained imported Roman-style goods
like a jug and pan designed for Roman ways
of preparing and serving wine.

75–25 BC
Aylesford, Kent, England
Copper alloy; H of bucket
34.5 cm
British Museum, London

Desborough mirror

In Britain 2,000 years ago people usually only saw their reflections in water, but a select few owned highly polished metal mirrors. The backs were often engraved with basket-weave hatching, creating complementary dark and light motifs. The care that went into the designs suggests that these were important objects. People may have believed that mirrors had the power to look into another world.

50 BC–AD 50
Desborough, Northamptonshire
Copper alloy; L 35 cm
British Museum, London

Decorated mount

The compass-drawn designs on this mount are so similar to those on mirrors from England that its appearance in a Scottish hoard must reveal connections between communities across Britain. Rivet holes suggest that it may have been attached to a wooden box.

AD 50–250
Balmaclellan, Dumfries & Galloway
Copper alloy; L 38.1 cm
National Museums Scotland, Edinburgh

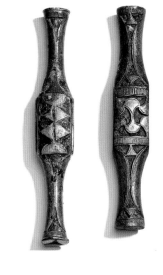

Sword scabbard (below)

In Britain, native warriors may have used Celtic art designs like those on this scabbard to stress their difference from the Romans. But this sword is not just a symbol of resistance. It was buried with others in a pit lined with fragments of imported olive oil containers, suggesting that their owners also aspired to Roman tastes. The materials used to make the sword itself also emphasise connections: ivory fittings on the hilt probably came to Britain via the Mediterranean.

AD 50–80
South Cave, East Riding of Yorkshire
Copper alloy, iron, enamel, whale ivory, elephant ivory;
L of scabbard 60 cm
Treasure House and Beverley Art Gallery, East Riding
Museums & Galleries

Chariot fittings

Horse and chariot gear was often elaborately decorated to attract attention and create a spectacle during battle. In regions of Britain where there was intensive conflict, people sometimes buried large hoards of chariot and harness fittings. Some were made from Roman-style materials like brass and included multicoloured enamel.

AD 40–60
Polden Hill, Somerset
Copper alloy, enamel; L of object below 14.8 cm
British Museum, London

Meyrick helmet

People on both sides of the conflict in Britain used Celtic art to proclaim their identities. The form of this helmet and the inscription on one side ('II' in Roman numerals) are Roman, but the decoration on the neck guard is typical of British Celtic art. Its owner may have been a local warrior who was serving with the Roman army.

AD 50–100
Uncertain provenance, probably northern England
(Collection of Samuel Meyrick)
Copper alloy, red glass; H 16.5 cm
British Museum, London

Dragonesque brooch

These striking brooches are now called Dragonesques because of their stylised, dragon-like designs. They show how local and Roman influences came together in post-conquest Britain. The design is based on an older S-shaped brooch style. In the Roman period, this simple native brooch form was sometimes enlivened with multicoloured enamelling.

AD 75–175
Uncertain provenance, England
Copper alloy, enamel; L 6.3 cm
British Museum, London

Armlets (below)

Although parts of Scotland lay beyond the direct control of Rome, peoples' lives were still transformed by Roman contact. Men wore massive armlets that could weigh over 1.5 kg each. These examples are decorated with long slender trumpet shapes, typical of the distinctive Roman-period Celtic art that developed in north-east Scotland. People north of the frontier wore these new designs to emphasise their difference from the Romans. Women and children wore smaller bracelets decorated in similar styles.

AD 50–200
Castle Newe, Aberdeenshire
Copper alloy, enamel; external
D 14.5 cm
British Museum, London

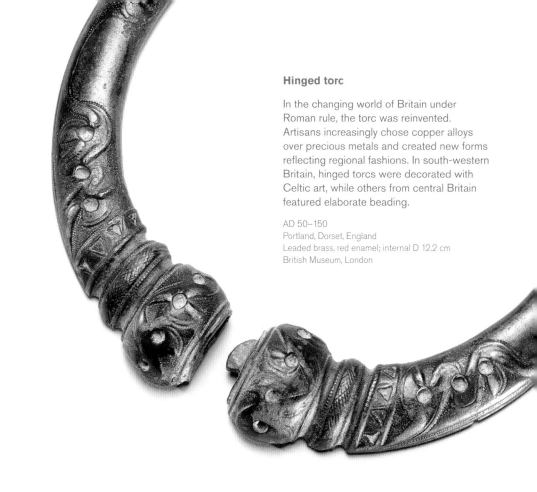

Hinged torc

In the changing world of Britain under Roman rule, the torc was reinvented. Artisans increasingly chose copper alloys over precious metals and created new forms reflecting regional fashions. In south-western Britain, hinged torcs were decorated with Celtic art, while others from central Britain featured elaborate beading.

AD 50–150
Portland, Dorset, England
Leaded brass, red enamel; internal D 12.2 cm
British Museum, London

4. A New Christian World

Roman control of Britain broke down after AD 410. In the south-east, Romano-British ways of life were gradually eroded as pagan leaders established Anglo-Saxon kingdoms. Even before this time, Scotland, Ireland and western Britain had developed their own distinctive regional cultures and identities. Interestingly, it was here – in the areas often thought to have been most insulated from the impact of Roman rule – that people continued to be influenced by Roman traditions, long after the army had departed. New styles of dress incorporated Roman-inspired jewellery, often made from recycled Roman silver.

Although the people of Scotland, Ireland and western Britain did not call themselves Celts, they spoke a family of languages now known as Celtic, which set them apart from their Anglo-Saxon neighbours. These communities also practised local forms of Christian worship. Monasteries, at places like Iona, became European centres of art, learning and literacy and provided an environment in which a new form of Celtic art flourished from *c.* AD 650.

Celtic-speaking artisans incorporated motifs such as spirals and three-legged triskeles into their art. But these were now combined with influences from the Anglo-Saxon kingdoms of England, particularly interlace designs. Although interlace is one of the most familiar features of early medieval Celtic art in Britain and Ireland, it has earlier origins and was used across Europe. Patterns of looped and knotted strands featured in Roman art, and later Germanic art.

Some of the most iconic Celtic art objects were treasures of the early medieval Christian church: richly illustrated gospels, monumental stone crosses and caskets for precious relics. The time and care involved in creating these intricate objects was itself an act of religious devotion.

In the medieval period influential families became keepers of sacred artefacts, including bells, books and crosiers. Some families commissioned ornate metal shrines for these objects, believing them to have the power to heal or harm. They sometimes carried the relics into battle. These families saw themselves as the guardians of history and tradition.

Pictish hoard

Roman silver came to Scotland, perhaps as diplomatic gifts, or as loot or payments brought back by returning mercenaries and raiders. This hoard contains Roman objects, like the silver spoon fragment, which was centuries old when it was buried, alongside locally made, early medieval items such as the pin. The spirals on the long pin are based on Roman-British Celtic art designs. The extraordinary leaf-shaped plaque combines Pictish symbols and spiral decoration.

AD 400–600
Norrie's Law, Fife
Silver; largest pin L 16.7 cm
National Museums Scotland, Edinburgh

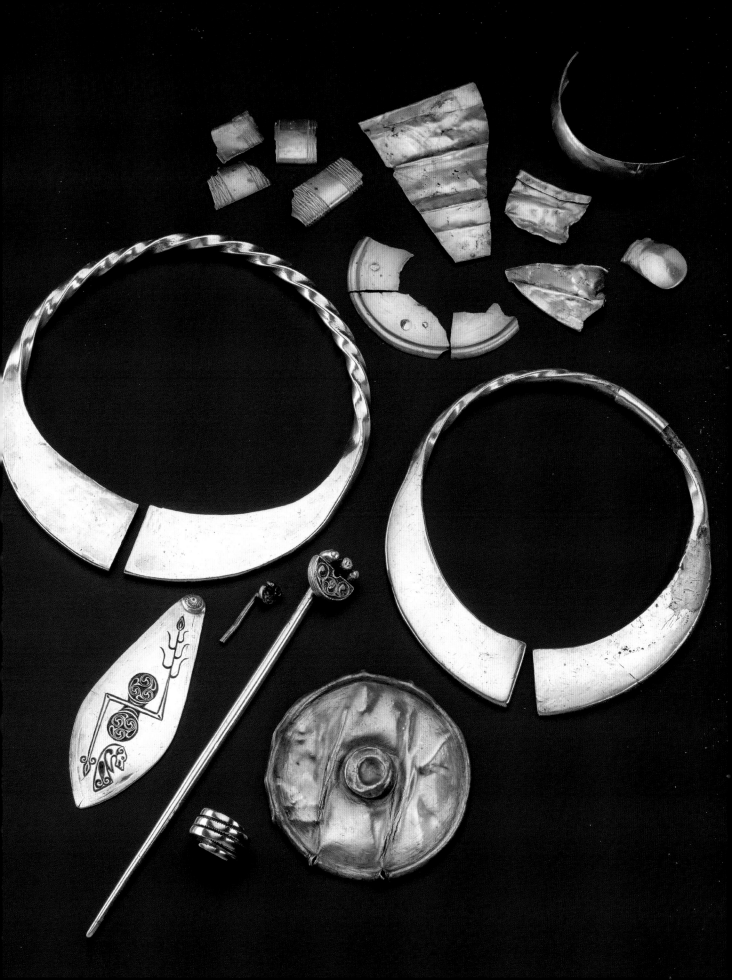

Londesborough pin

Large decorated silver pins were a new
and distinctive type of object made in early
medieval Ireland, Scotland and western
Britain. The decoration on the shaft of the
Londesborough pin was inspired by older
Celtic and Romano-British art.

AD 400–500
Ireland (unknown provenance, Londesborough
collection)
Silver, enamel; L 32.8 cm
British Museum, London

Sutton Hoo bowl

Treasured luxury items reveal the flow of art
and ideas across Britain. This hanging bowl
was part of an exceptionally rich Anglo-Saxon
ship burial in eastern England. But it was
not locally made. The use of red enamel and
interlocking bird-head motifs suggests that
it was imported from the Celtic-speaking
regions of Britain and Ireland.

AD 610–640
Sutton Hoo, Suffolk
Bronze, enamel; D 29.8 cm
British Museum, London

Tully Lough cross

Churchmen may have paraded this cross during Christian ceremonies. The metal panels draw on a range of influences. Some illustrate biblical stories, such as Daniel in the lion's den. Others are decorated with patterns: interlace from the Anglo-Saxon world, and scrolls, trumpet shapes and bosses inspired by earlier Iron Age and Roman designs.

AD 700–800
Tully Lough, Co. Roscommon, Ireland
Bronze and gilt bronze over tinned bronze backing plates
(wooden form is reconstructed); H 127 cm, W 43.8 cm
National Museum of Ireland, Dublin

Donore disc (above)

A hoard of metal plaques buried in Ireland included this finely carved disc. The plaques were probably attached to a church door or casket before they were carefully removed and concealed. The combination of trumpet shapes and three-legged swirls shows a fusion of earlier Celtic art and new Anglo-Saxon influences. Many of the same patterns can be found in the detailed illuminations in contemporary manuscripts.

AD 700–750
Donore, Co. Meath, Ireland
Copper alloy, tinned; D 13.1 cm
National Museum of Ireland, Dublin

St Chad Gospels (overleaf)

Elaborately illustrated gospel books played a central role in the early medieval church. Monks devoted hours to painting the intricate designs that highlight important passages. The extraordinary craftsmanship and the range of influences are clear on the pages of the St Chad Gospels. An initial letter, marking the opening of the Gospel according to Luke, encompasses three-legged swirls and crescent shapes that owe much to earlier Celtic styles. Geometric motifs echo Roman designs and interlace inspired by Anglo-Saxon art. The right-hand page features a cross densely filled with interlaced birds and beasts with elongated twisting limbs.

AD 700–800
Lichfield, Staffordshire
Vellum, pigments; H 30.5 cm, W 23.5 cm
Lichfield Cathedral

Hunterston brooch

The form and decoration of this brooch show
a dynamic mix of influences. It was found in
Scotland, but has the form of the closed-ring
brooches that people preferred in Ireland.
The front is covered with interlaced beasts in
intricate filigree (beaded wire), a technique
from Anglo-Saxon England.

Two of the small panels on the back of this
brooch are filled with spiral designs, an earlier
Celtic art motif. This finely worked decoration
would have been hidden when the brooch
was worn. Centuries later, a new owner
added the inscription 'Maelbrigte owns [this]
brooch' in Viking runes.

AD 650–750
Hunterston, North Ayrshire
Silver, gold; D 12.2 cm
National Museums Scotland, Edinburgh

St Ninian's Isle mounts (left)

These small objects were part of a hoard found under the floor of a church. They feature the characteristic patterns of early medieval Celtic art. One is decorated with spiral decorations and three-legged triskele patterns, the other is covered in twisting interlace.

AD 700–800
St Ninian's Isle, Shetland
Silver, gilding; H 4 cm
National Museums Scotland, Edinburgh

St Ninian's Isle chape (right)

The St Ninian's Isle hoard may have been a church treasury buried for safekeeping or the wealth of a local aristocratic family. Some of the objects, including silver bowls, may have had a religious purpose. Others were secular symbols of power, like sword fittings. This is a chape, the protective fitting from the bottom of a sword scabbard.

AD 700–800
St Ninian's Isle, Shetland
Silver, gilding; neck W 1.3 cm
National Museums Scotland, Edinburgh

Rogart brooch

The Rogart brooch includes finely crafted details showing feeding birds. Birds drinking from fountains were a symbol of eternal life in Christian art, demonstrating the religious meanings of many apparently secular objects. The brooch is also covered in intricate interlace designs.

AD 700–800
Rogart, Highland
Silver, gilt, glass; D 12 cm, pin L 19.3 cm
National Museums Scotland, Edinburgh

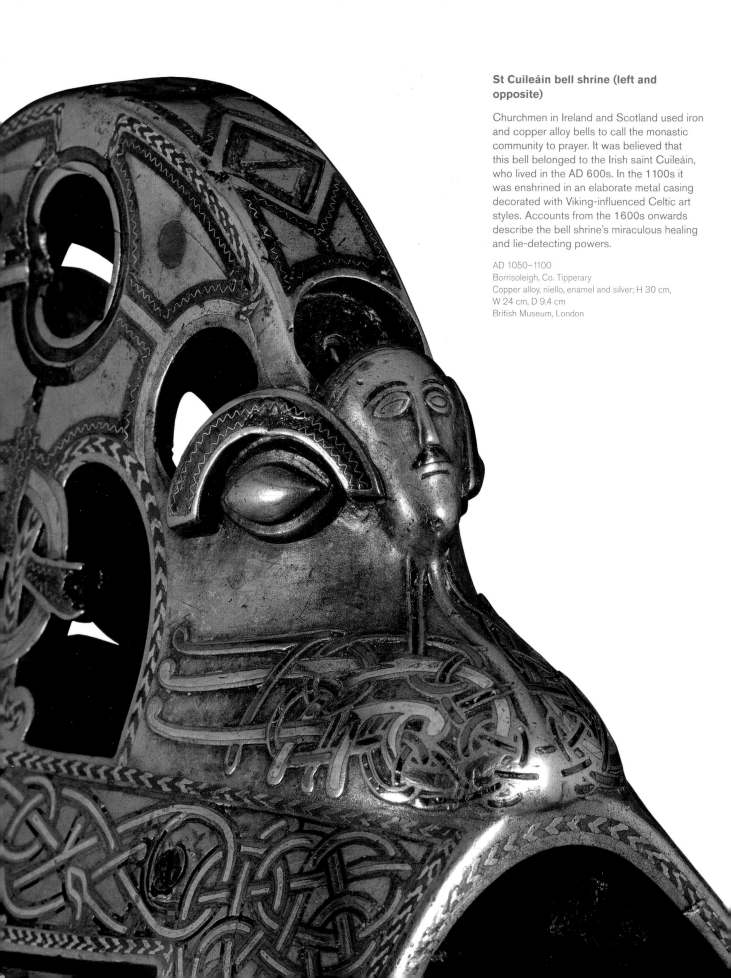

St Cuileáin bell shrine (left and opposite)

Churchmen in Ireland and Scotland used iron and copper alloy bells to call the monastic community to prayer. It was believed that this bell belonged to the Irish saint Cuileáin, who lived in the AD 600s. In the 1100s it was enshrined in an elaborate metal casing decorated with Viking-influenced Celtic art styles. Accounts from the 1600s onwards describe the bell shrine's miraculous healing and lie-detecting powers.

AD 1050–1100
Borrisoleigh, Co. Tipperary
Copper alloy, niello, enamel and silver; H 30 cm,
W 24 cm, D 9.4 cm
British Museum, London

Monymusk casket (right)

The front of this small casket is inscribed with faint animal interlace, while the red enamelled hinges and mounts are decorated with scrolls and interlace. It might have housed the relics of a saint, although it is now empty. Little is known of this object's history but it seems to have been preserved by influential families in Scotland for many generations. In earlier times, its owners may have believed the holy reliquary held the power to heal or harm.

AD 700–800
Kept for many years at Monymusk House, Aberdeenshire
Silver, copper alloy, gilding, glass, enamel and wood; H 10.8 cm, W 9.8 cm, D 5.1 cm
National Museums Scotland, Edinburgh

5. Renaissance and Revival

During the fifteenth century, the developing nation states of Renaissance Europe began to look for ways to understand their past. There was a renewed fascination with classical Greek and Roman texts, some of which referred to the ancient Celts. Over the following centuries, the term Celt, which had fallen out of use after the Roman period, became commonplace and was applied to the early inhabitants, languages and monuments of western Europe, and in particular to those of Britain and Ireland.

Artists depicted Celtic peoples, showing them as the fierce warriors described by Greek and Roman authors. But their weapons and appearance were often inspired by those of indigenous peoples encountered by European colonists at this time. The absence of Celtic art is unsurprising as many of the artefacts shown in this book were found only later, during the Victorian period. It was in the 1850s that these objects were first called Celtic art.

In the nineteenth century, new archaeological discoveries fired the public imagination and inspired contemporary jewellery designers to make their own versions of ancient brooches. The popularity of Celtic-style jewellery was fuelled by royal patronage. Interest in Celtic art led to a movement known as the Celtic Revival, part of the wider Arts and Crafts movement, which promoted traditional crafts in response to the industrialisation of Victorian Britain. Some artists from Ireland, and from northern and western Britain, deliberately drew inspiration from thousands of years of archaeology, history and myth to create a romantic vision of the Celtic past.

The Revival influenced politics as well as art, feeding strongly into modern identities in Ireland, Scotland, Cornwall, Brittany, Wales and the Isle of Man. Communities here drew on their heritage to articulate their difference from the English and French. Today, these nations share an idea of common ancestry and tradition. Celtic art has played a role in this development, but we should take care to understand the various histories and contexts of objects made during 2,500 years of British and European history. We must untangle the jumble of Celtic objects that were consciously combined in a work like John Duncan's *Anima Celtica*.

Pictish warrior holding a human head

Watercolours by the English colonist John White were among the earliest attempts to visualise the ancient people of Britain. Completed following a voyage to North America in 1585, they combined elements inspired by indigenous North Americans with descriptions of the ancient Britons written by Caesar and other authors, to show perceived similarities between these groups.

John White, *The True Picture of One Pict*
From Thomas Hariot, *A Brief and True Report of the New Found Land of Virginia* (1588)
Watercolour touched with bodycolour and white over graphite; H 24.3 cm, W 17 cm
British Museum, London

Brooches (overleaf)

In the mid-nineteenth century, competing jewellers trawled libraries and museums in search of Celtic designs. An early medieval brooch from Ballyspellan in Ireland inspired a smaller Victorian version set with garnets. The replica piece was acquired by Prince Albert during the royal visit to Dublin in August 1849 and given to Queen Victoria as a Christmas present. Royal patronage helped to popularise Celtic jewellery and design.

Top brooch:
c. AD 900
Ballyspellan, Co. Kilkenny
Silver; L 25.2 cm
National Museum of Ireland, Dublin

Lower brooch:
1849
By Edmund Johnson for West & Sons, Dublin
Silver, garnets; L 13.6 cm
Royal Collection Trust, London

Celtic Revival vase

Artists and designers exploited the fashion for household objects embellished with patterns based on ancient Celtic art. Archibald Knox designed this vase and a similar tea set for the department store Liberty in London. Its interlacing decoration was inspired by the Celtic art that he saw on stone crosses on the Isle of Man, where he lived.

1906–9
Pewter; H 29 cm
Victoria and Albert Museum, London

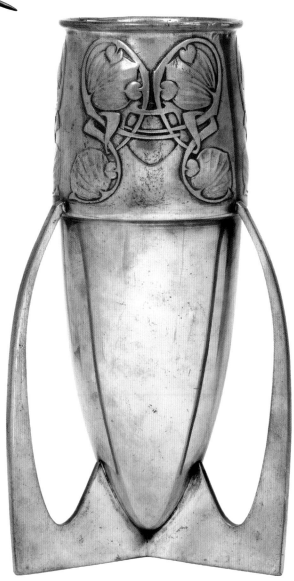

Anima Celtica (opposite)

John Duncan's illustration for Patrick Geddes' journal *The Evergreen* blends elements from 3,000 years of history and archaeology in a single timeless image. A dark-haired woman conjures up scenes of a mythical Celtic past. She wears an open-ring brooch (*c.* AD 800) and an armlet (*c.* AD 100). In front of her lies a Bronze Age sword (*c.* 800 BC), and an eighteenth-century Jacobite dagger. Around her are standing stones from deep prehistory, the heroes Fingal and Cúchhulain from early medieval Irish tales, and the blind bard Ossian, who was invented by James Macpherson in the 1760s. Duncan combined these to create a romantic vision of what it meant to be Celtic in the Victorian era.

John Duncan, *Anima Celtica* (Celtic Soul or Celtic Mind)
From *The Evergreen, Book of Spring*, 1895
Image H 22.5 cm
National Museums Scotland, Edinburgh

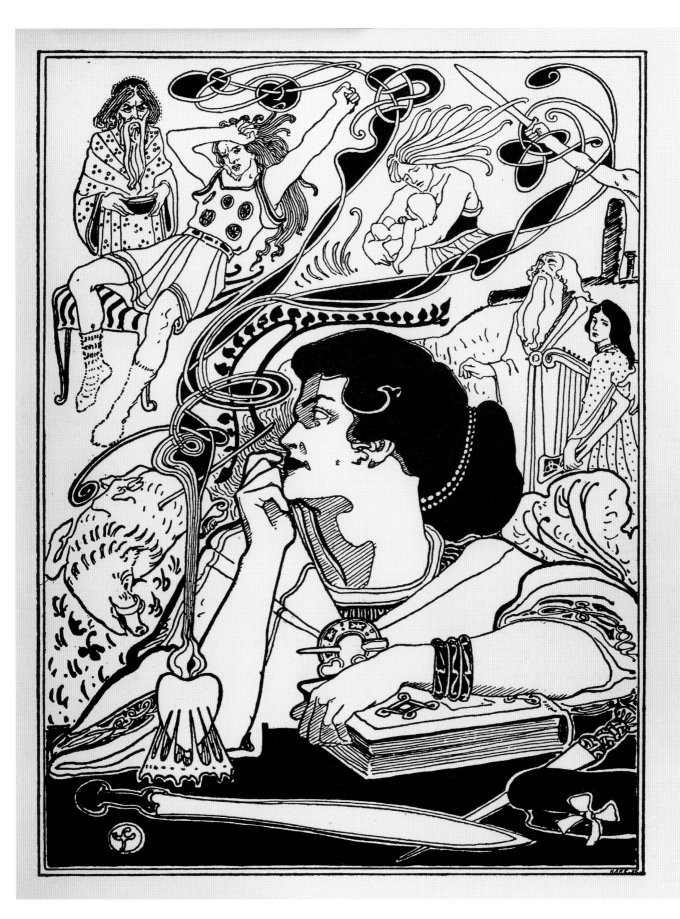

Acknowledgements

With special thanks to Julia Farley and Fraser Hunter; Frances Fowle, Martin Goldberg, Jody Joy and Heather Pulliam; Rebecca Penrose; Rosie Weetch; Maggie Wilson; the photographers at the British Museum and National Museums Scotland; Coralie Hepburn, Kate Oliver, Axelle Russo-Heath and Will Webb.

Bibliography

Brown, M. 2015 *Art of the Islands: Celtic, Pictish, Anglo-Saxon and Viking Visual Culture, c. 450–1050.* Oxford

Collis, J. 2003 *The Celts: Origins, Myths and Inventions.* Stroud

Cunliffe, B. and Koch, J.T. (eds) 2010 *Celtic from the West. Alternative Perspectives from Archaeology, Genetics, Language and Literature.* Oxford

Farley, J. and Hunter, F. (eds) 2015 *Celts: art and identity.* London

Garrow, D. and Gosden, C. 2012 *Technologies of Enchantment? Exploring Celtic Art: 400 BC to AD 100.* Oxford

Gosden, C., Crawford, S. and Ulmschneider, K. (eds) 2014 *Celtic Art in Europe: Making Connections. Essays in Honour of Vincent Megaw on his 80th Birthday.* Oxford

James, S. 1999 *The Atlantic Celts. Ancient People or Modern Invention?* London

Megaw, R. and Megaw, V. 2001 *Celtic Art from its Beginnings to the Book of Kells* (revised and expanded edn). London

Stead, I. 1996 *Celtic Art* (2nd edn). London

Wells, P.S. 2012 *How the Ancient Europeans Saw the World: Vision, Patterns, and the Shaping of the Mind in Prehistoric Times.* Princeton

Youngs, S. (ed.) 1989 *'The Work of Angels': Masterpieces of Celtic Metalwork, 6th–9th Centuries AD.* London